ARMCHAIR THEATRE

ARMCHAIR THEATRE

Brian Docherty

For Jeremy
with best
wishes,
Brian Doc
4/3/07

Hearing Eye

First published 1999

○ *Copyright Brian Docherty 1999*

ISBN 1 870841 59 X

Published by Hearing Eye
Box 1, 99 Torriano Avenue London NW5 2RX

This publication has been made possible by the financial assistance
of the London Arts Board

Typeset by Emily Johns
Cover by Emily Johns
Printed by Catford Copycentre

FOR ROSEMARY

You just go on your nerve

Frank O'Hara (Personism: A Manifesto)

Some of these poems have appeared in the pamphlets *The Andy Warhol Happy Hour* (Special Sorts Press, 1991) and *Ventriloquism* (Hearing Eye, 1991, reprinted 1993)

Acknowledgements are due to the editors of the following magazines and anthologies: *ABSA Annual Report 1990*; *The Argotist*; *Anarchist Angel*; *Catatonic Extra*; *The Echo Room*; *The Exile Poetry Competition Anthology* 1993; *Fat Chance*; *FEDeration*; *First Time*; *Foolscap*; *Fortnight*; *Gairfish*; *Iota*; *Jugular Defences* (Oscars Press, 1994); *Main Street Journal*; Mother Earth Journal; *New Statesman & Society*; *Not the View*; Poems On The buses; *Poetry Now London 1994*; *Poetry Now London 1998*; *Red Lamp*; *The Reader*; *Riding Pillion: The Poetry Business: Anthology 1994* (Smith/Doorstop); *Scriptor; Smith's Knoll; Tees Valley Writer*; *Under the Asylum Tree* (Survivors' Press, 1995); *Various Artists*; *Verse*; *Vertical Images*; *The Wide Skirt.*

'Come Ashore Jacky Tar And Your Trousers On' was a runner-up in the Jersey Eisteddfod Poetry Competition 1995; 'Virtuoso : John Ogdon 1937-89' won 2nd Prize in the Muswell Hill Library Campaign Poetry Competition; 'The Muse' was a prizewinner in the Exile Poetry competition 1993; 'Sure It's A Grand Old Team to Play For' won 2nd prize in the Tees Valley Writers Poetry Competition Spring 1994.

CONTENTS

PURPOSE/PARABLE

If there is a purpose to writing
other than counting the slaves or tallying
the rents, these wars, these plagues, must be
the news that stays news. Gather all the tribe
in one field, you can repeat till they know
then take it home for the children. *Long ago
and far away,* you invent Uncle Oscar's life
for them, myths and codes to keep them safe.

Mother's mischievous helpers walk the world,
Hanuman, Anansi, Coyote, Loki, leaving their card,
new world, old world, third world, all one
to them, an ancient game they never
tire of. They change the rules when Mother
isn't looking, blame everything on the humans.
They argue about which one don't have
the Buddha nature, do a good deed or two.

COME ASHORE JACKY TAR AND YOUR TROUSERS ON

When I was a wean my grandfather told me
tall stories about his grandfather.
"He wis a sailor, went roon the world
five time afore he wis twentyone."

"Once he wis shipwrecked on Mauritius,
him an' fortytwo o' his mates survived sharks,
thrown back on the beach like drookit rats.
They made the Dodo extinct, ate anythin' that moved."

When I was twelve I went to the Kelvingrove,
a whole Education in itself, better than school.
What caught me was this enormous crab from Japan,
a genuine monster the size of a soup tureen.

I told my parents about the mediaeval armour,
the dinosaur skeletons, the French paintings,
the rocks in the case that glowed in the dark.
The crab was my secret, I went just for that.

Twenty years later it scared me even more.
I thought about Captain Cook in the Pacific,
pinnace full of scientists, official artists,
ambitious middys. Beach full of *Machrochiera*.

"Catch me one of them DAMN YOUR EYES step lively."
Barefoot tars slipping and sweating on coral,
oars and nets, man-long legs, hand-size pincers.
"Hells Bells how d'ye catch a thing like thon?"

"Belay that shillyshally you sons of Bitches
or it's an hundred lashes for every manjack."
How many lost fingers toes the arse of their breeches
or suffered gangrene then amputation on the table?

Did they get a pension for what they lost
or a fine for tearing their uniform,
while the scientists, cold rationalists, sat snug
planning learned articles and lecture tours?

Fiddle and squeezebox in the fo'c's'le
    'Hey ho chicken on a raft
    O what a terrible sight to see'
needlework and scrimshaw for the nimble.

They held their peace when the whores lined up
on the Broomielaw to wave and sing out
Come ashore Jacky Tar, wives and sweethearts
later, "a CRAB did that? Och yer arse."

THE HAPPY GENIUS

Who shall say I am not /the happy genius of my household?
('Danse Russe',William Carlos Williams)

We picture Williams as stubborn old man
tapping out poems with his middle finger
electric gesture to the world
releasing his words like pearls
torn from the depths of his brain.

This is one scene from a long movie
truer than Henry James patronising Hardy.

Yes, they produced their best work
at an age when most men give up
yet they were once young and vigorous
great lovers of music and dancing.

There is a photograph of Williams
about the time he wrote 'Danse Russe'

handsome

        elegant

                sensual

what an eyeful

        the neighbours must have got

what dance did he do for them?

ecstatic Hasidic whirling

        rustic Morris dance

                proud Flamenco syncopation

something American perhaps

    hoedown

        buck and wing

            Charleston

Dr Williams delivered 5000 babies
his poems were a public scandal

      50 years of Rutherford life
          went into his surgery
              come out in the poems.

"There's a lotta bastards out there"
his prognostic to Jack Kerouac 1957.

They never had the measure
      of the Satyric Doctor
          who desired every woman he met.

THE ANDY WARHOL HAPPY HOUR

Being famous was easier in Shakespeare's day,
your chances were 10 times better at least
and you probably got more than 15 minutes
even allowing for disease, illiteracy, the censor.
At my first public reading poets outnumbered audience;
not quite fame but we enjoyed our 15 minutes.
My lift home strands me at the edge of the world
timing the last bus in footstamps till a drunken
Irishman sprays his small miracle on my briefcase.
I whack him in the balls with my uncollected poems.
Auden was wrong; poetry matters in the most immediate way.
A passing police van takes him to the Whittington.
"What happened to you Sunshine, hit you
with an anapaestic tetrameter? Assyrian was he?"
On the 41 I remember another Irish piss-artist
in the Queen's Crouch End who hailed me:
Allen Ginsberg! bought me a pint for quoting 'Howl'.
Then my image of Ginsberg was a 60s freezeframe,
now his *Collected Poems* photo scans dentist, lawyer,
but for the gleam in the eye, open to everything.
I too have a suit, a tie, a pair of black shoes,
but wear that disguise less often than Ginsberg
who became 'the Poet' in my year of discovery, 1967.
How did that stranger intuit the connection
years before Ginsberg cut his hair and beard,
I started doing readings, even admitted to 'poet'?
Now he chants Blake songs, meditates sex and death,
I do politics / humour / social comment, even love poems.
Like our photographs we meet in the middle,
moderate men who avoid the authorities.

DID I REALLY SAY THAT?

Every poet is their own Secret Police
the plain buff folder in the hidden drawer,
remind us we could write *that sort of stuff*;
back then a source of shy pride not shame.

The best Christmas present I could wish for
three poems in a workshop magazine.
They were raw as Beaujolais Nouveau
Och well it's the thought that counts.

After End of Term drinks I go to Dingwalls.
In the mirror I mimic a Company agent
shades briefcase fedora cowboy boots.
I could sell a mountain of coke tonight.

The lady with the ready-rolled joint
gives me lessons in rhythms and blues
up on stage Dave Edmunds & Nick Lowe
belt out *What Did I Do Last Night?*

Camden Lock moonlight has frozen 'Home'
to an ideological construct I gesture
to my companions *when I die I want to be
reincarnated as a ladies bicycle saddle.*

2 am and the taxis can't stop won't stop
the police are auditioning the Bow St. Panto
Jim and George get booked as *Drunk & Disorderly,*
I get off scot-free Och well Ah would.

THE ART GAME

In the alternative universe of art classes
I'm a little spaceship caught in a gravity field
held against a black velvet background
making music in my head to pass the time.

In the break I come to earth,
play explorer, witness to new creations;
over there a good likeness of *me*
suspended in mid-page like a UFO.

The artist has abolished
gravity context history
Mrs Thatcher couldn't do better.

Just the thing to impress dinner guests.

Hey man that's good Yoga
who's your teacher?

I like Vermeer, his dark richness,
the confidence of the Dutch bourgeoisie.
An evening class tutor told me the secret:

"I'll tell you what he was about,
the hidden bats only seen from certain angles;
them merchants used to get their friends round,
give 'em a big dinner, get 'em pissed."

How many can you see?

That, Madam, is paint.

VIRTUOSO: JOHN OGDON 1937-89

At nineteen we knew all about music,
genius was Ray Charles or Pete Townshend;
in our electric world Clapton was God.

Sunday night was suit-time in the *Golden Eagle*,
learn to behave, drink Pernod and whisky
little bhikkus trying the world for size.

Then our inscrutable well-connected friend
brought a special friend to augment our sangha,
enormous round Bodhisattva showing Right Speech.

He came among us like the blue-eyed stranger
with no history that we knew of
and a famous name that meant nothing to us.

By the exaggeration of respect MR John Ogdon
could have been a 33° Mason to provincial boys
untried at measuring beyond our own horizon.

Nobody guessed the long exile in the Maudsley,
the piano a therapy tool between brain-frying sessions
editing out false notes in the mind's chatter.

The piano was always in the corner
an instrument of fixed and equal temper
solid and reliable in a world of shadows.

Fifteen years later he looked just the same,
shuffling onto his Birthday Concert stage,
a holy fool seated at his shrine.

Now he has walked to Cold Mountain,
his music is the light of the full moon,
a gift of clear water to guide the traveller.

A FRIENDS OF THE EARTH MEETING, DEC 1989

For a change they have poetry and music,
make jokes about saving the world then read poems;
the string quartet play a slow movement from Haydn.

The violinist is Jewish, *eine shayna maidel*,
she insists "This is not *Deutschland Uber Alles*".
Pull the other one, friend.

I remember the last time I heard that tune,
a Catholic church in Schwarzwald's border country;
my friends knew the hymn. The Other? Who knows?

Now 'Grosse Deutschland' is on the agenda again,
they are knocking through the wall
in our common European home.

Words like 'Anschluss' and 'Lebensraum'
stand to attention
as the Bundesbank prepares to annexe Prussia.

In the beerhalls little men with Lugers
insist it is their tune
as their children squabble in the greenhouse.

Washington and Bonn have sold us to Japan,
now they will sell everyone in Eastern Europe
a Big Mac and a Coke while *Für Elise* plays endlessly.

When the Fourth Reich has its housewarming party
the Agents will be proved right. Extensive grounds.
Spectacular views from Silesia to Slovenia.

THE PROBLEM OF FORM IN MODERN POETRY

Behind the Puzzle Factory is a wall
a blue plaque says Harry Stottle lived here;
we get the guided tour from Tom or Sydney
(or someone of that kidney) who points out

the Arts Council-sponsored line of plastic palms,
the Grove was sold to a pencil factory

In the garden there is a small
(or large) pool of uncertain aspect

It is difficult to be certain in the gloom,
our host has talked for a very long time

"It is said there are pearls in this pool
        it is a local legend
you can have one attempt only
but you can try as long as you like"

We kneel in a circle round the rim
stick our arms and /or heads into the murk

        "By the way there are also
        electric eels in the pool"

"Sonnet writing class this way in five minutes"

Down by the river Old Uncle Bob Cobbing
explains the difference between concrete
poetry and concrete boots to a visiting Martian

What's that? Answers? Not my Department, John.

THE RED HAND

Cuchulain dips every newborn brain in blood
so that both halves will remember their history.

I asked my friend why he left Ulster
"I know forty words for light rain."

Ignatius Loyola and John Calvin could equally
love a language so subtle yet rigid.

Stranded on the wilder shores of dogmatism
bellowing out *The Sash My Father Wore*

While at a party a stone's throw away
Sean South and Roddy McCorley live again.

It is always 1690 or 1916, 1926 or 1969
according to your understanding.

The ghosts are hungry for blood tonight
as the rough beast slouches up the Falls Road.

Who was that Masked Man
silver bullets will not suffice in this darkness.

On the 15th August 1969 the Army came
at five o'clock in the afternoon.

The Army came to the streets of Belfast
at exactly five o'clock in the afternoon.

Welcome to Sunny Ulster.

IT MUST BE TRUE

I heard it on Radio 2 in the *Friendly Foodstore*
would Jimmy Young tell a lie over the air?

"20% of the population have pain every day
a survey reveals that men can stand pain
better than women." Here in the studio . . . .

Who did the survey, under what conditions?

Are we a nation of masochists
Are you a registered Masochist
Are you now or have you ever been
a member of the Sadistic Tendency
Have you enjoyed 13 years of Thatcherism?

What sort of shoes do *you* like
What's your favourite sort of uniform?

Can *you* tell the difference between
a prison in Britain and one in Turkey?

Would you rather be an oppressed minority
in a) Belfast   b) Jerusalem   c) San Francisco?

If *you* could be a policeman anywhere
in the world which State would you choose?

Put that thing away you're making me
                nervous

I've never seen one like *that* before
please don't do that   please
         more more oh oh YES!

ARMCHAIR THEATRE

We've all played the game of
"Where were you on 22 November 1963?"
tried to describe our grief.

How would the Mafia and the FBI,
the patriotic Klansmen, do on that score.
"It's all a matter of perspective, boy."

A united front of the ruling classes
guns and uniforms and a dead hero.

We had ours with Churchill soon enough
the first State funeral on television.
While the English commentary spoke for Britain
I went to the Tally's for icecream and lemonade.

A man lurched out of the 'Hawthorn'
"Deid at last, deid at last,
th' auld bastard's deid at last."

Making it sound like a cry of freedom
one more link in the chain broken.
Was he remembering Tonypandy 1910
when Churchill sent in the troops.

Or Sidney St. where the Home Secretary
turned up with his personal Tommy gun;
the General Strike and the British Gazette
and Churchill's words to the nation.

We are at war.
We must go through with it.
The Strike must be crushed.
These words from an 'A' level textbook
published by Harold Macmillan's old firm.

Richard Dimbleby mentions none of this
as the First Lord of the Admiralty
rides his last gun-carriage through London
surrounded by the Queen's Navee.

Down at Waterloo Station sits Engine 34051
Winston Churchill, Battle of Britain class;
the corpse has his own train
steaming to his final anchorage.

"Haw see this Armchair Theatre, it's garbage,
turn ower tae the White Heather Club."
Almost anything is preferable
provided it speaks in our own tongue.

PAST PERFECT

The spare room presents me history in a packet,
old snapshots achieve the status of movie stills,
flashback to the distant games of childhood,
imagining your family as filmstars.

Dad as Kirk Douglas with a normal chin
Mum as Marilyn Monroe in a caravan door
Willie as Fred Astaire in mechanics overalls
Nana as Katharine Hepburn in a biscuit factory.

1960 features a little boy, a red bike, a Zorro sword;
with my astronaut crewcut and summer tan, everyone
said I was a little American. Bugs Bunny, peanut
butter, the Celtic Supporters Club in Kearney N.J.

10 years later my single ambition was a two-reeler
crossing the Golden Gate Bridge on a Harley Sportster,
an extra in the decade's blockbuster, advertised
in *Rolling Stone* with a Grateful Dead soundtrack.

TV documentaries make the Fifties another planet,
Joe McCarthy and Roy Cohn made Nixon look clean;
if they were humans no wonder the Russians
were Martians in 'B' movies. Heroes to villains.

Rock'n'roll, Bebop and beatniks became threats
to Middle America's moral fibre. Ugly small-town
minds couldn't take Kerouac, Presley, Brando
all at once. And the women, that Marilyn Monroe.

Now the Sixties look equally strange on screen,
Woodstock reduced to a quaint costume drama;
did we really quote the *Little Red Book* imagining
roles in the remake of *Battleship Potemkin?*

SURE IT'S A GRAND OLD TEAM TO PLAY FOR

He is watching American football on TV
"Ach nuthin' but a buncha big Jessies."
His friends call him 007 or Mac The Knife
looks like Sean Connery licensed to kill.

He argues the virtues of real football
the woman next to him slaps the bar
"Pele, Eusebio, they were men, but the rest ,
Mariconas, you know? I prefer American style."
.

The bell marked *Attraction of Opposites* rings
for both but chemistry overrules them.
Her cousin met many like this in Lisbon
after the football in 1967. Complete with kilts.

"Yes Maria, they came for the European Cup
their Celtic playing Inter Milan in Estoril
so many who never went home again."
This one left after the Revolution.

His boss shifted operations to Rio
he has no passport no permit no problems
goes to Colombia or Paraguay, does his job
drinks in bars where English is spoken.

Scotland is a fading memory of rain, tenements,
outside toilets. He has trouble with his wife's name,
his weans, Thomas aged 8, Suzanne aged, *whit?*
They must be older than he was when he left.
.

MARTIAN DELTA BLUES

Today's radio mixes music and memorials
twenty years ago Hendrix crashlanded
skip search / memory bank / Summer '67

Top Of The Pops darkens my father's face
trying to decode the Hendrix drawl
was that "Kiss the sky" or "Kiss this guy?"

Either way I don't care   that's my song
flashback/ first hearing / Cream's *I Feel Free*
stranger change than puberty done without drugs

Family jokes about changelings make sense
if I sprouted antennae and turned green
it couldn't match the brain chemistry.

Now *Purple Haze* charges the breakfast air
I eat my mushroom omelette with ginseng tea
shaping up to do the weekend shopping

Strolling round Spaceship Sainsbury's
seems sort of . . . . . different somehow
even the uniforms are brighter and tighter

"Good Morning this is Captain James T. Kirk
welcome aboard the 10am service to Mars
we hope you have a pleasant trip . . . ."

Uniforms surround me "Walk this way Sir
stowing away is a VERY SERIOUS OFFENCE"
OhshitI'msoconfused / I LOVE YOU Lt. UHURA

*Seenyour sort . . .   manytimes . . .   affront . . . decentsociety
. . . business . . . . protected . . . . commonthieves . . .
suitabledeterrent . . . reports . . . Planet Broadmoor . . .*

THE REVOLUTION WAS TELEVISED LAST NIGHT
The revolution will not be televised: Gil Scott-Heron.

Ronald Raygun, Acting President? Absurd.
Hollywood would never film that scenario;
'smalltown boy goes West, makes good,
Big Business buys him the Governor's chair'.

They liked his role in McCarthy's movie
throwing the commies out the Actors Union.
They re-appeared as B-movie Martians
Invasion Of The Bodysnatchers their comeback.

America elected an autocue pilot
primed to mumble anything to order;
when the extras got adventurous
his memory was exposed and found blank.

Czechoslovakia elected the scriptwriter
Havel's actors the vanguard of the revolution;
this time round Uncle Joe's Travelling Circus
would not throw them off the stage of history.

In the Paris Maydays Danny the Red cast
the Stalinist carworkers as his vanguard
he should have signed up Bardot and Belmondo
offered M. Hulot the part of President.

Starwars a flashback to smalltown certainties
the Military/Industrial Complex will survive
to sell everyone in China one of everything.
Their Man In The White House will see to it personally.

THE MODEL'S TALE

Doesn't pay much   but useful anyway
help apprentice artists learn their trade.
(where would Henry Moore be without models)
Big anatomy charts   bare muscle bone
skeleton illustrates me   tutor lectures
Iliac crest   pit of the throat   bony structure.

Locked on the block unable to move
they approach sticks scalpels garottes
ready to torture me into new shapes.
Sheer physicality fascinates.
Lunchtime a dubious relief   my kidneys
pass a colour coded health warning.

Get dressed be a person again for an hour.
Mirror tells me I'm too old for this game
Canteen offers standard institutional stodge
jeunesse doreé rehearsing tomorrow's triumphs
mature students silent purposeful disciplined
They are *in* but not *of* this circus.

National Student shock articles on facing pages
refinements of torture Ulster Chile South Africa,
Tories say *Cuts Necessary, Arts must be relevant.*
Answer me: how does this place stay open?
Then a sick thought   who trains torturers?
How do you become an apprentice torturer?

How horrified our liberal lecturers would be
if their students were trainee torturers
State sponsored to develop *creativity.*
How better to learn than a sculpture course
perhaps a little poetry on the side
practice *dissociation of sensibility.*

EASY WITH THAT KNIFE

What it comes to is *grace under pressure*.
As my father would say "Manners maketh the man."
Example, what to do when you go to meet the boss,
your wife's uncle, your brother's boyfriend.

"Don't laugh at his haircut for godsake."
A pudding-basin parody of shortback'n'sides.
I'm thinking Retro Chic till I notice
this 2 inch square bare patch on one side.

Has he had a secret operation
or gone to the barbers on a bad day,
asked for a *Tony Curtis*, got handed the
Lon Chaney Victim of Science model?

You don't dare ask about alternatives.
Another example of Victorian Values,
the return of the Barber-Surgeon.
Hold him down while I see to his neck.

Sweeney Todd was a model of efficiency
compared to 'Figaro' the Calton Barber-Poet,
who wrote songs to order for his clientele
of Music-Hall Artists; the ones they liked
survived generations of Glasgow audiences.

Drivin' intae Glesga on ma soor milk cairt
leaves a better taste in the mouth
than Thatcher's knife above our throats.
I'll stand a sentimental love song any day
before the swinish chorus of *Greed is Good.*

WHEN IN ROME . . . . . EAT THE RICH

Having abandoned the Empire and duty
they made war on the populace for XI years
led from the front by a new Volumnia
the staff of office a rod for our backs.

Rumours of war among our masters
we will learn whose *patria* it is
ours who do the dying in foreign wars
or theirs who lisp "dulce et decorum est."

They have bought us with false coin
sold us what was ours already
we will teach them the difference
between 'subject' and 'citizen'.

The lictors have bound themselves like *fasces*
thrown the Leaderene over the cliff
in the villa a warm bath is waiting
the wolves will gather to shit on her grave.

They do not understand this notion of 'elections'
some Greek business to benefit provincials
not a real patrician among them
more choice in a butcher's shop on fire.

We who elected her with acclaim III times
are denied a voice in this debate
we remember our founders with love
we will have a Republic of Wolves.

VENTRILOQUISM

The voice in my head is a pine tree
the voice I speak with is a telegraph pole;
did I talk different 10 years ago?
Older poems taste rusty in the mouth
as if written for another voice.

I want poems to fill the mouth
like granary bread hot with the bellybreath
Blake's *process of unconscious dictation*
nutty and sweet as a pint of stout.

I hear myself described as a 'London Scot'
by a Party hack who balks at 'working-class'.
Anyone who owns the *Complete Works of Joseph Stalin*
must have an ear for the proper note;
Modernism & Cosmopolitanism have their limits.

Even Lenin who applauded Isadora Duncan
was bourgeois enough to phone Lunarchevsky
"Mayakovsky's gone too far this time
          have him flogged!"
Mind you, Stalin was right about Shostakovich.

I have been down here 16 years
of slowmotion vowels and blended tongue,
about the time from the October Revolution
till the Moscow Trials reprised the old song.
          Time to eat the evidence.

I never wrote them Your Honour
I find you Guilty Of Everything
ye'll be nane the waur fir a hingin'
Stalin would have liked Justice Braxfield.
Free Speech? One each afore ye go.

DERBY DAY 1991

Enter any branch of the University of Life
any cultural historian will tell you
"Nijinsky, oh aye, great horse son, great horse,
gied thae bookies a right scunner."

We discuss the great names of the past,
Mill Reef, Hill House, Arkle, Sea Bird II,
Fokine, Karsavina, Pavlova, Markova;
one name stands out in both worlds.

He means the greatest son of Northern Dancer
whose grandson Generous came in at 9/1
reeled in by the shouts from the stalls
the only one whose stamina matched the stage.

I tell him Vaslav Nijinsky's story,
10 years of glory before he turned
from Diaghilev. "The little horse is tired."
30 years tethered to Tolstoy's ideal.

"Oh Jesus. That's terrible son. A pure waste.
At least the horse got put tae stud."
Vaslav's daughter never danced; his heir
Nureyev gave millions generous pleasure.

We discuss genealogy. I say Bronislava
Nijinska's ballet dances London this week.
He tells me he saw Nureyev and Fonteyn on TV.
"Brilliant. Ye never forget somethin' like that."

AUGUST 1969/JUNE 1991

I remember the week I was 16
but not if that August was wet or fine
old enough to know what was going on
but not able to go do it or be it.

The Sixties arrived late in Scotland
television our window on the world;
two events three thousand miles apart
where rain blurs a million muddy hopes.

The Army invaded Bogside then Belfast
half a million people taken prisoner.
In Woodstock half a million achieved
synchronicity: *three days of peace and love.*

If the God-fearing people of Ulster
had realised they were the next Vietnam
would they have called the Starship Enterprise
to beam them over to the States?

In revolt against majority morals I was
hungry for the gift of flesh accepting flesh
finally realising most people are in fact
completely naked under their clothes.

Some are shrink-wrapped aged 7. .
Can you imagine Ian Paisley naked?
Neither can he. *Save Ulster From Sodomy.*
No Surrender to the modern world.

The murder gangs are out again tonight
politicians play footsie under the table
the Jim Morrison movie fills the screens.
Altamont & Bloody Sunday drowned our dreams.

AMANDLA !

Last night among my dreams
sparkled this beautiful thought:
'the new flag of free Azania
will be a Nelson Mandala'.

Next thing I am translated to a commune.
South African hippies. I don't believe it.
Guitars, drums, goats, two acres of *boontjies*.
It's like Wales with flowers and snakes.

Forty people and only six surnames,
worse than a Welsh pit village.
Everyone has the same story;
"my father / uncle / brothers" : *verkrampt.*

They're secret surfers hiding from history.
Every seventh wave is white. Politics is boring.
The townships are a long way away.
Of course they support the ANC.

We pass round a stick of Malawi grass,
cans of Lion. Later we get the munchies;
"all I got is this strip of *biltong.*"
It tastes tougher than a Boer's boots.

In comes the born-again Christian
I met in Spain. ("Blacks are not people").
So much for the transforming power of love.
400 years of history proved too strong.

The cat censors my dream.
He paraphrases J. R. Stephens on Chartism;
"a knife and fork question." Then Brecht,
"grub first then ethics." *I want mine now.*

FREUD FOR BEGINNERS

Where do poets go after a reading?
Straight to the pub of course,
suck the top off a pint of lager.

Parked in a booth with two drunks,
one Irish one Geordie chant cantifable
telling each other gamey stories.

The Irish one takes his turn:
"Y' know my sister has 3 kids
well I was round there one day.

The two eldest were small 3 or so
they were in the bath together
Brid was down in the kitchen.

She hear all this screaming
Mammy mammy mammy come here
went up the stair to witness murder.

'What's all this row then?'
Little Patrick points and bawls
Frances has lost her willy.

Jesus I laughed and laughed
he's grown up now married himself
every time I see him I bring it up.

Shurrup he says *Shurrup.*
Brid says 'Well you're a big boy now'
Shurrup Shurrup the pair of you."

As I take my leave at 11 o'clock
Geordie faces two pints of Old Sheepdip
Irish sucks his empty bottle of Extra Stout.

AUNT ANNIE'S CARD SCHOOL

Taking the bus to Finsbury Park tube
we read the railway bridge's livid cry
POLICE MURDERED GEORGE JOAKIM 18/4/91
GLR announces the Maguire Family's appeal.

16 years' struggle summarised in 2 minutes
Guildford 4 Birmingham 6 Maguire 7
3 of a kind cards marked for life
all cheated of an even chance.

1974. An average evening in Kilburn
a family grouped round the table
hands greasy with cards and money.
This home video switches to *The Sweeney*.

"We got a full house here Sarge
we come up trumps this time alright
I'd say this looks like a bomb factory
make a nice headline in *The Sun*."

In the station sense is beaten into
their stupid Irish heads. Bang to rights.
They made the bombs for those bastards
In Birmingham and Croydon. Didn't they.

The bomb Squad celebrates a prial of 3's
their best score ever. Old hands lift the pot.
A Judge impartial as any poker tourney referee.
They have been caught in the act. Haven't they.

14 years on the word of a lab technician
dealt back into the pack branded GUILTY
the youngest 13 years old half a life ago.
Money will not give him those best years back

Truth can be bent like a rubber truncheon
plausible as any pretty policeman
plying his trade in Earl's Court or Finsbury Park
or searching for IRA hard men in Kilburn.

The priest named cards the Devil's Picture Book
now his sermon strikes truth from homily
cards and horses less of a wasted life
than eating shit in a foreign jail.

Conspiracy takes 2-6 people somewhere private
a police van or a card school for example;
organised crime is where power and money meet.
Send a bomb squad to the Stock Exchange.

A tramp tries a citizens arrest on us
his red weeping eye a broken sunset
his voice a scratchy 78 playing 'Sixpenny Money'
20p an insufficient bribe to let us go free.

His hand is an excavator clotted with filth,
like Joyce's it has done a lot of other things.
Perhaps he is an undercover policeman
digging up the dirt among the bogwogs.

Stroud Green's Irish Centre faces an African grocer,
two cultures joining hands in a strange land.
Legend claims the Fomor made Ireland from Africa;
in this foreign field they fight the same fight.

Some have been foreigners in Finsbury Park
long enough to recall the 50s bleakness
NO BLACKS OR IRISH the card dealt to them,
the landlady always had a Full House.

WHAT WERE YOU DOING DURING THE COUP?

I was enjoying my holiday in Glasgow,
a week with my family away from London.
Edinburgh? Nice town, shame about the people.
The Festival? The TV highlights were enough.

How many alternative comedians does it take
to tell a joke? 400. 2 to actually tell it,
3 to research the material,395 to act as
the audience. Canned laughter courtesy of Holsten.

Here's 1991's in joke, for reference only
you understand. Don't nick it.

"Have you heard the latest about
The Bank of Crooks & Coke International?
If you go to their cash till
you get a choice of 3 services

A wodge of cash
                a lump of hash
                            a Kalashnikov rifle."

John Maclean would be first in the queue
followed by Boris Yeltsin and V.I. Lenin.
One to educate the workers in capitalism
one to show them how to enjoy their freedom
one to show them how to deal with nationalists.

A POSTCARD FROM ST. PETERSBURG 20/8/91

Perhaps the old Tankies think if they
do it in August we won't know or care
or by the time we realise Winter will
have set in. By the Spring the trials
will be over. The ground will have thawed

Enough to do the burials. Things move faster
now. Eight days and it's all over for now.
They have enough order and discipline left
to make up their own personal firing squad.
No need for awkward questions anymore.

And now the ones they hate most, the liberals,
the radicals, the nationalists, will do the rest.
Carry out the CIA's programme for them. Unpaid.
Of course the American people don't understand
Imperial Russia was most of the Union anyway.

Think of America minus the nastier parts
of the Deep South. That's Russia after the breakup.
Not much of a loss *tovarich*. We can live without
the fundamentalists. So could you buddy. You bet.
Mirror images. We even have a Georgia each.

The same people who founded Kiev in 980
live in your Mid-West. We had an Empire
before your Puritans learned to feed themselves.
Tell your children about the Great Patriotic War.
Our history is long. Do not turn your back on us.

FALLING IN LOVE (AGAIN)

Seven seconds of terror is all it takes.
The French have a word for it,
coup de foudre: lightning strike.
Hormones dance among the brain cells.

Testosterone. Phenylethylamine.
Riot of the heart. Tygered in the night.
If love is a revolutionary act
I want to be your comrade in arms.

Blood bangs the idiot xylophone
beating the message into the head
desire a durable and dissonant music
tuned into unison by our bodies' concert.

Comfortably past the seven year itch
my motto this year, back to the basic Tao:
avoid the authorities. Look after the roses.
We have achieved a home and jealous neighbours.

Contributions will be made and given
in different ways. Less meat. More flowers.
New hats from Tibet and Guatemala.
Give up modelling. Subscribe to magazines.

Our garden is full of wild surprises
the piano pours out its music
the TV blew up so we write poems
the cat wants to be my copy-editor.

The view from my desk is Ally Pally
the BBC mast a mini Eiffel Tower
monument to the work of another Scotsman.
Genius is such a useful romantic concept

"I love you" the ultimate state of egoism
like Caspar David Friedrich's little man
in a big landscape arms embracing the void.
I want it all, such a greedy pleasure.

I prefer those endless Chinese scrolls
where the monks and merchants go their way
no big deal no trace of their passing
their poems made with brush and rice wine.

Freedom is the row of French marigolds
I planted yesterday. Orange and green
symbolic colours from India to Ireland.
Every day with you an exotic pleasure.

My editor is asleep. I am free to write,
read this to friends, 'challenge the gantry'.
I have already embraced the moon.
Loving you. How could there be another life.

ROUND UP THE USUAL SUSPECTS

The *Hornsey Journal* has a column called 'Crime Shorts'.
No, it's not a modern version of the striped jersey,
the sack stencilled SWAG. A list of those caught
in or after the act. Sundry neds, villains, psychos.

This week's haul has Gerry Conlon, Paddy Armstrong.
Couldn't wait, could they? Bailed for possession
of cocaine & Ecstasy. Perhaps they got the habit
inside. Or they're that sort anyway. Take your pick.

Funny isn't it. They get out, do something silly.
Remember George Davis, the campaign to free him?
He couldn't wait either. Caught in the act
with a shooter at the Allied Irish Bank. Old habits.

Everyone is equal in the blind angel's theatre.
Stick a sawed-off in a bank clerk's face,
stick a coke-filled bank-note up your nose,
the law proclaims you equally guilty. 14 years.

The man in the mutton-chop whiskers, the wig,
the 18th century mind, has the power to throw
away the key to your future. A menace to society.
Thrust back into the belly of the beast.

You have no right to the rest of your life.
It is harder than ever to avoid the authorities.
The hyenas will camp outside your door
whether you are logged in Largs or Tufnell Park.

Writing books is not a good idea. Live quietly,
take a menial job. If you go to the pictures
a voice will call you up later. "We will rape
your corpse & eat the evidence." Be a good boy.

LOVE AS A FOREIGN LANGUAGE

To celebrate their 2nd year at Trent Park
Eric and Keith went cruising through France.
They were drinking citron pressé in a bar
talking Foucault and Bataille as students do.

A regular came in for a Pastis 51, and to
read about the Tour de France's progress
then he noticed the two strange men.
"I see you have some intellectuals today."

M. le Patron looked across the counter
put his towel down. "No they're English."
This seemed a good time to drive to Marseilles.
"God they're worse than the lecturers."

They cruised into a chrome palace
populated with Marlon Brando parodies
where an innocent expression like *bugger me*
could lead to the biggest thrill of your life.

One half of the bar was Triumph riders
the other half Harley fans discussing piston
positions and lubrication. "This is more like it."
Rough trade the same all over. *Read the manual.*

They met two Scots clones from London;
tartan and leather is so romantic cheri.
"Come doon the Swinging Sporran sometime
we'll show ye whits under a Scotsman's kilt."

You can't have a holiday romance in Islington
café breakfasts a *Cage Aux Folles* farce.
None of your sauce about bent croissants.
They did enjoy the drive home. *Piston positions.*

GETTING YOUR CARD MARKED

Why no Xmas Card from Oscar this year?
On Boxing Day I phone to see how he's doing.
A strange cold voice snaps 'He's not here'
as if acting in a 3 minute opera.
I call on a mutual friend from college
to get the story. It takes several drinks.
He's in the Hospice his family refuse to visit.
His lover died 6 months ago in the next bed.

The toilet door rehearses popular opinion:
ARSE   INJECTED   DEATH   SENTENCE
save a marriage hang a lesbian today.
On the stroke of 8 a disco blasts out.
The locals reckon we don't belong here.
Drink up. Tell the 6 shell-suits round the table
our spaceship leaves in 2 minutes. Gandhi was right
Western Civilisation would still be a good idea.

"Like living in a Breughel painting"
his opening line on entering the Hospice
now he remembers his grandfather's words,
"look for the light within you",
hoards his speech for the necessary moment,
plays Satie's *Gymnopedies* for the other guests.
Any song you care to mention has too many memories.
I force myself to say I will visit *soon.*

This morning I meet Jane at Seven Sisters,
3 minutes while commuters swirl round us,
both late for our last class of term.
She meant to write: Oscar took a *long* time to die.
His family rallied round at the end.
I change Tubes to go discuss Marge Piercy,
themes of sexual freedom, abortion, women's choice.
Dylan's *Tears of Rage* ringing through my head.

Break the rule about lunchtime drinking. The pub
radio drops casual facts between Springsteen tracks,
'The virus tricks healthy cells into killing themselves,
in the US 1% of the male population are affected'.
Fuck your statistics, Mr DJ, Mr Scientist,
we are all living on borrowed air
we are fallen angels whose balloon has burst ,
back to earth from our hormone high.

Jane gives me the William Burroughs version
of the Gaia Hypothesis. 'We are an invasive parasite'.
An expensive mistake. *Abort this programme.*
Mother is indulgent till we want too much.
Impatient with excess out comes the Kali mask,
syphilis, influenza, or try something new.
Mother Nature has the biggest stick of all
to punish naughty children. *All Fall Down.*

MUSIC ON THE TUBE

A day so dreich the buskers have abandoned
the tunnel's echo chamber for pub or betting shop;
they could play out their skins for Irish pennies,
no share of the salaries headed for Covent Garden.
The Piccadilly Line packed with that payday look,
or are they really timing the run to Heathrow
in case the wrong lot win the next Election?
I want some Impromptu Theatre to empty the seats.

Then I notice they are not counting stops.
A cellist exploits his captive audience,
lectures them on politics between phrases,
bowtie and manic eyes echoing Paul Tortelier,
grips his cello like a lover, dreams of du Pré.
Was he inspired back in the Sixties by her passion.
Does he remember the little girl by the radio
calling out *That's the noise I want to make.*

Say *cello* to some people, they respond 'Casals';
for my generation cello is Jackie du Pré,
the golden girl our lector cannot forget.
I thought he was showing off for some girl;
from my restricted view seat I cannot tell Bach
from Dvorák, work out which party he is abusing.
What lesson is he giving us this wet Saturday?
At Arsenal a double-bass player plunks on.

He embraces his instrument, does not undress it,
smiles his way to Holborn, waltzes his bass away.
By King's Cross an old lady has had enough.
"Two nutters in one carriage is too much,
he got on at my stop." Who was the other one?
Two Guardian Angels join the audience,
one stop later they've had a beret-full.
Playing music in public is not illegal. *Is it?*

Memory strikes in like a held chord;
a BBC2 documentary on du Pré's life,
her ardent performance of Elgar's Cello Concerto
then a 1979 scene from a Master class
after multiple sclerosis stole her career;
the angry woman in the wheelchair who could
just about lift her hand to her pupils:
That's the noise I want to make.

RODIN'S *MUSE* FIGURE

Rodin old Master old goat
scorned for most of his life
famous too late to change
followed the grand tradition
of exploiting his models, put
them into impossible positions
let them walk free about
the studio, caught each moment
when he could. When Whistler's
memorial was commissioned
Gwen John was the model of choice.
The biographies footnote her as
sister of Augustus, model for Rodin,
star pupil at the Académie Carmen.
Scientific application of colour
was Whistler's gift to the quiet
woman from Wales whose interior lives
have outlasted her brother's bombast.
How many visitors to the Musée Rodin
seeing that armless plaster cast
modern Venus de Milo monument of love
know the work she did in Meudon
unconcerned with fame or fashion.
There are no men in her pictures;
cats nuns peasant girls Augustus's
wives, standing alone and silent.
Did she feel abandoned by her Master
after he had taken what he could
confident he had immortalised the woman
he made love to in the cupboard?

HERNIA DIARY POEM

Squelches when palpated. Nil by mouth. A minor
procedure. Nothing to worry. Home by 4 pm.
Shortcuts show when I have to shave myself.
My hernia is a large egg in a muslin bag.

Into the lift like bread into an oven.
The anaesthetist looms over the operating table
"We call this *happy-juice,* some people think
it tastes like garlic." *Sail away to Xanadu.*

Pain drags me over the reef to Cannibal Beach.
Fire in the belly eats me alive, boils me down.
Painkillers allow me the luxury of impersonating
Bing Crosby or Howling Wolf. *Miserable bastard.*

Nurse runs through her 1 day op. spiel about
disabling the femoral nerve. "Don't worry it wear
off soon just do the exercise we told you."
While I drift a ghost dog is stealing my leg.

4 hours later I'm the 1% who can't walk home.
Two nurses lead me round the ward then step away.
My knee crashes to the floor like a peasant girl
having a vision. Not what the Buddha meant by *letting go.*

Getting out of bed demands ingenuity and will,
going to the toilet becomes an adventure.
Clenched teeth and a hand on your valuables
will take you a long way on the Deathrow Shuffle.

My Generation blasts through the hospital radio.
Pete Townshend was right. Death before decay,
this beautiful machine wearing out & no trade-in.
I've seen the future today. Take it back Mister.

BODHISATTVA

Every morning he comes to my bed
shouts 'MU' in my face
if I fail to wake up
he knocks my glasses to the floor.

He has the large ears and round belly
that denote a compassionate nature
he applies his stamp to my writing
rebukes me for reading books.

When he is hungry he eats
when he is thirsty he drinks
if there is a fire in the room
he sleeps before it.

If he hears Mozart or bebop
he listens with perfect indifference
if he hears reggae or heavy metal
he covers his ears or leaves the room.

He understands the basic Tao
if he sees a uniform approach
Gas Postman Police Insurance Man
he runs *avoiding the authorities.*

He answers to the noise 'Andy'
if it does not interrupt the work
of being himself. He has ways to say
'We are equals I shall ignore you'.

The edge of the world is 100 yards away
it is always NOW   right   HERE
he does ordinary things nothing special
his life is not an example to anyone.

CATS AGAINST NUCLEAR POWER

They are an elegant exercise in perfect timing
they can even make millions for mediocre composers
prancing women in painted leotards a pale imitation
denying Old Possum's grinning skull beneath the skin.
We never hear their mating cries in the garden
they do their fighting and fucking somewhere else.

As a child in Glasgow that noise terrified me
convinced it was the souls of lost demon children
rising up the walls of our tenement to the kitchen
window, to hang there, inviting me to join them.
I prayed they could not make me get out of bed.

Do you remember that film *Children Of The Damned*
their red eyes shining power and command
taking over dull 50s England with ease.

Does your cat order you about with superiority
confident of who is the master race
rebuking you for not anticipating his every wish.

Having seen a Scottish wildcat rip open
a dead sheep, I am thankful our little masters
from Egypt and Lake Van are like Napoleon
small but perfectly formed, garden size gods.

I sleep well at night, untroubled by evil
I hardly notice the nuclear trains passing
through on the line at the bottom of Crouch Hill.
I believe the scientists who say it's safe.

But my cat stays in at night till it passes
he knows how small things die in the night
wakes me up when it crosses Hackney Marshes
believes water is barrier to anything unnatural.

BROKEN LAWNMOWER BLUES

It broke the weekend before I went into hospital.
I obey the doctor's injunction against heavy work,
watch roses and wildflowers frame the grass,
unable to bend or stretch to cut them back.

The cat carves a path through the wilderness,
his long swerve of lust into the night.
For once he has a proper hunting space,
somewhere to pursue his private business.

Today with this 'energy efficient' mower from Argos
I can restore this decadence to suburban propriety.
Time to get the gardening togs from the shed.
As usual Andy paraphrases Thoreau on economy.

He is perfectly dressed for every occasion,
does not flinch when the shears clack round.
He demands a throne be built from the ruins.
While he rests the mower steals his grass.

Tomorrow he will complain when it is bagged,
today he is a miniature leopard, mighty hunter.
Every tree on his territory has a new nest.
He will visit them all to test his power.

If I am lucky he will bring me a present
his eyes shining with triumph. "Look Stupid."
I will settle for having the garden back
even if he would prefer a mockup of Lake Van.

Next door's fishpond is covered with netting.
He will accept milk from Mr Young instead,
ancestral memories of freshwater fish receding;
garden size gods accept any tribute they can.

SUMMER COMES TO CROUCH END (MAYDAY)

The street is graced by cherry blossom
tomorrow rain will mash it to a muddy paste
we are strolling towards summer's mirage
already LA & Sarajevo's promise is *long, hot.* . . .

Can't happen here? You have a short mind.
Broadwater Farm is only a bus ride away.
Which bitter name not yet burned into history
is this year's Handsworth St. Paul's Toxteth?

MayDay strange voices phone for improbable girls
then 5 calls in 3 hours from friends:
"Bastards nicked the TV/video/hifi/Apple Mac";
"OK which carboot sale do we hit first Saturday?"

I give the Jehovah's Witnesses my 'Jesus was
a Commie faggot' routine then threaten to read
my epic poem ' I Fell In Love With A Lesbian'.
That always takes the shine off their shoes.

They have been trained like Chinese cadres
The enemy anyone who answers back. Try telepathy:
Take your redemptive bibles somewhere needy
you drove past the frontline to get here.

We are shedding our surplus clothing
take your attitudes away from our bodies
take them to those rancid housing estates
where rags are being stuffed into bottles.

Friday morning wipes it all away
Ally Pally smeared out of the landscape
the artist impatient with London's perfection
a week of sun more than we deserve.

SUSPENDED SENTENCE

They opened a file as soon as I appeared in print,
a red star and a yellow sticker meaning 'Trained at
The Anglo-American School Of Typewriter Wrestling'.
I am on parole after 6 months writing Latin epigrams.

I have given my word to mind my language
no more going equipped with Pound & Williams.
I have agreed to write proper English Verse
like Masefield & De La Mare, stay away from Bunting.

The Judge's dictionary has lots of words.
Recidivist. Flaneur. You know the sort of thing.
If I offend again I will be exiled to a place
where the language has no word for *pyjamas*.

I will not use foreign words
not even the ones we stole from other languages.
I will not make my typewriter commit unnatural acts.
I will not spill my politics on the paper.

The Poetry Police are beating out a rhythm
on my door, trochaic tetrameter paraphrasing
Beethoven, *Thus Fate Knocks At The Door*.
Read ma badge. You're huckled ya wee clype. BELT UP.

They have brought a chair with straps, a copy of
*The Dodo Book of Dead White Middle Class Chaps
From Oxford*. They will either bore me to death
or re-educate me to be a useful citizen.

They had a spy taping last night's reading.
"I'll read some new work" came out as
'These words are a conditional discharge
to stain your fingers and pollute your mind'.

THE VOLCANO GOD'S SONG

Our volcanoes are the Campsie Hills
pimples on the acne'd face of Scotland
most people in Glasgow think *Ring Of Fire*
a Johnny Cash song about rednecks in love.

Santorini and Vesuvio are Italian restaurants
Krakatoa one of the 10 worst films ever made
Mt. Pinatubo sounds like an Australian wine
Radio 4's gothic description tells more.

"An environment of total darkness and mayhem"
worse than Sauchiehall St. on Saturday night.
Sky God sang *Abolish these little silver birds*
Volcano God sang YANQUI IMPERIALISTS GO HOME.

Clark Air Base emptier than a communist coup
Manila trembles, 60 miles suddenly a short distance
10,000 bars stripped of the Yanqui dollar
All Shook Up a bad joke on the juke-box.

Subic Bay has more warships than 1942.
The Unions sing out "Give us our wages."
No money for 3 weeks : no rice on the table.
Nothing is free in paradise. Not even freedom.

Real power shifts around the Pacific Rim
clear & present danger in every corner
four continents around the fracture zone
a shifting alliance of tectonic plates.

The arrogant chatter of global politics
has left the Holy Loch a peaceful backwater.
Some general listened to his totem animal
Leave the poison dwarves alone. YANQUI GO HOME.

WHATS IN FRONT OF YOU: A RIDDLE

I am long and slim and tilting
full of something you want
I am red and green and pointing
to the part of your future

You are afraid of but desire
helplessly, eyeing me constantly
through the window. If you think
about it, you cannot afford me

You will hate yourself next
morning, your children will
despise you for bringing me home

Say to their friends they will
not make me welcome in their homes
when they are old enough to choose.

(A bottle of red wine)

RITE OF PASSAGE
(for Steven Constantine)

When I was 15 I deserted the local Youth Club
for the Air Cadets, rejecting the Sea Cadets' kit.
I was smart with promise, thought the Sergeant.
He offered me the chance to use a real gun.
Was I officer material, a 9 year sign-up?

He led me through the red light onto the range.
He handed me weight, purpose, responsibility.
Real cartridges, a man sized target bobbing up.
Suddenly all those films like *Guns of Navarone,*
those *Sergeant Fury* comics, the little *Commando books,*
were shown up for what they were. Playground stuff.

That gun, those cartridges, the Sergeant's orders,
that shaky target, were the very things to click
'reality' into focus; squeezing that trigger,
watching that painted torso sprout holes,
thrust my childhood into a cupboard of the mind.

A long step on the road to being a man,
for a moment my future focussed through
the barrel of a gun, an Audie Murphy
awaiting orders, no matter what they were.

The Sergeant's bark pulling me towards
responsibilities, complicities, the khaki itch
on my groin the right feeling to have,
the tightening finger, the narrowing eye,
showing the Sergeant I had the makings.

ABUSING THE LANGUAGE

In most countries *macho* means guns & cars.
In Scotland it means wearing a garishly coloured
dress & a purse, designed & made in Lancashire for
Queen Victoria's holiday. *Traditional Your Majesty.*

In 1973 when Aberdeen was translating to Oil City
the Inland Revenue sent me to the College of Commerce.
Business Studies to make me a tougher tax collector.
How did you think the NHS & nuclear subs were paid for.

The tweed jacket teaching Behavioural Science
informed me I was an *invert.* Hans Eysenck said so.
I thought he was saying I had an attitude problem,
realised he was hinting he knew I was a Jessie but
wouldn't go public. 1967 passed him by all round.

Business English took us to the pub the last night,
wore Y-Fronts under his kilt, kept grunting things:
"Ah'm a Mountain Man & Ah like mountin' wimmin."
I expect he got that one from the *John Brown
Book of Traditional Witticisms For All Occasions.*

When Sheikh Yamani raised the cost of living
the SNP started bleating about 'Scotland's Oil'
looking to Norway as exemplar of independence
strutting about with skean dhu's down their stockings

Now they turn out to all the anti-racist marches
denounce the National Front as an English import
howling they are good Europeans & multi-culturalists.
But leaning over the farmyard gate in Perthshire
old habits die hard. Civil rights for keelies? *No Chance.*

PUBLIC THEATRE

As public theatre revolutions are hard to beat.
In Paris Robespierre took centre stage while
in *another part of the wood* Australia's first play
was being performed in Sydney Cove by convicts.

HMS Sirius transferred a stock company
of poachers trade unionists Irish rebels.
Aboriginal theatre lost actors audience venue
to smallpox. Lights out overnight, no refunds.

Corpses were stacked like crocodile hides
so much stage lumber left like the aftermath
of a corroboree that went on too long.
The dingoes cleared the stage afterwards.

Their lives were worth less than the sheep
used to teach them the meaning of 'pastoral'.
Life is not a three-walled room to show off
theories about estrangement or alienation.

Neat labels for what we do to entertain
all those nice people in the bosky suburbs,
Glasgow Bristol Liverpool, living on the interest
of the profits from their ancestors' adventures.

200 years later and the money still rolls in
while their children go off to university
learn the mantras: *Colonialism & Imperialism,*
join the SWP & Troops Out   cash Daddy's cheques.

They think they can pay their dues in commitment
as if political economy were really that simple,
the elegant electronic dance of money & ideas
round the network too fast to be seen or stopped.

CALL ME UP IN DREAMLAND
(For Robert Creeley)

Down a long book-lined corridor
I hear my grandfather's voice
sharp and strong as the life
coast to coast on the Shaman Radio.

Is that a real poem
or did you make it up yourself?
Then my mother at Xmas to Rose,
Well he doesn't get it from us.

Forgetting her father's playful stories
Si senora deredego forti loris inaro.
I remember his alcove toolroom
dark oil odour neat racks of tools.

The corded muscles hard as experience
every word shaped and weighted
fit for the purpose he announced
every gesture precise to its own line.

I like to think I resemble him
but know I am still the 'prentice boy
too much loose talk and hasty hand
always close to spoiling the job.

I am too late to win his approval
journeyman on a road to nowhere
head full of things the hand has not mastered
trying to go beyond what I absolutely know.

WHERE I GO IN MY DREAMS

The place in the dream is familiar,
a sepia scene where the trams turn
in a circle in the Vienna Woods.
I have never been there in real life
any more than say, San Francisco,
another city I could navigate via films
or reconstruct stone by stone from books.
I have a strong and aching memory
of leaning against the rear rail
of the tram talking to a pretty girl.
In Dutch she would be *gezellige*.
I cannot think of the German equivalent
nor what her name might have been
even though we had just kissed,
might have been lovers, our soundtrack
a Strauss waltz, called I believe,
Geschichten aus dem Wiener Wald,
the narrative borrowed from Kafka
or Freud as you choose. The clothes
make it pre-war, but which war,
the sepia tinge implies nostalgia,
slow tempos, good manners, not Harry Lime's
shifty paranoia. As dawn approaches
I know the film is running out even though
I am still asleep. I hope to meet
this girl again, learn her name, perhaps
take her father for a beer, but for now,
the tram starts up again, she steps off,
and walks away not looking back
up the moonlit road running into the woods.

WHAT'S IN A NAME

I am standing on Platform 3 when they approach
They have been watching me watch the goods wagons
trundle past going somewhere commercially sensitive,
SEACOW SEALION DOGFISH GRAMPUS stencilled on the side
Who thinks up these exciting names and was he paid?
Was he sent round Dogger Lundy Fastnet Rockall,
to collect enough names for every type of waggon,
Why not SHARK BARRACUDA MANTA RAY DOLPHIN
or would that raise false expectations,
glamour, performance, exotic drugs in every car?

NO. We deal in everyday reality, dull lumpy names
to shunt commerce all over the franchise. We will
keep the sexy names in a drawer for the morning
after Privatisation, then get the workforce out
with the rags, the wire brushes, scrub the past away,
along with the Unions, the salary scales, the grading
structures. A new brush will be applied in every sense
my friend, and if it gets in your eyes or up your nose
that's too bad. Now bugger off, this is Private Property,
you are in my cost centre and the dobermans are hungry.

FORGET any drug references, you know what's good for you,
these wagons did not come from Amsterdam or Marseilles.
I have a friend who has a contract already signed,
to build a jail and own & operate several old ones.
He has a list of trade unionists and types like you.
Get on your train while you can still afford it,
we will not be running this enterprise for the
likes of you, nor the people on the housing estate
you won't walk through at night, although they may
benefit from access to what we might be transporting.

IF YOU know what's good for you, hire a video,
buy a six-pack, order up a pizza, lock your door.
My colleagues are modelling the new uniforms
for the Security Force in your area. Very impressive,
don't you agree. My name? *None of your business Sunshine.*
You'll have a chance to get a good look at them soon.
They will be coming your way, their way, call it what
you like, that's our privilege now that we have
bought this country from the previous owners.
I don't care where you live, this is your train.

For a complete list of Hearing Eye publications, please write enclosing an SAE to:

Hearing Eye, Box 1, 99 Torriano Avenue, London NW5 2RX